THE BIRDS OF MISSISSIPPI

poems by

Liz Glodek

Finishing Line Press
Georgetown, Kentucky

THE BIRDS OF MISSISSIPPI

Copyright © 2016 by Liz Glodek
ISBN 978-1-944899-53-0 First Edition
All rights reserved under International and Pan-American Copyright Conventions.
No part of this book may be reproduced in any manner whatsoever without written permission from the publisher, except in the case of brief quotations embodied in critical articles and reviews.

Publisher: Leah Maines

Editor: Christen Kincaid

Cover Art: CC0 Public Domain

Author Photo: Quyen Dac Nguyen

Cover Design: Liz Glodek

Printed in the USA on acid-free paper.
Order online: www.finishinglinepress.com
also available on amazon.com

Author inquiries and mail orders:
Finishing Line Press
P. O. Box 1626
Georgetown, Kentucky 40324
U. S. A.

Table of Contents

About the Poems 1

Welcome the Birds.. 3

M_____.. 4

Georgianna... 5

Emily Harrison 6

Abby Anderson.. 7

She Whom the Worms Loved.. 8

Little Mary 9

Katie 10

Rebecca 11

Mother Shaw 12

Another Woman, 42.. 13

Annie... 14

For Alice

About the Poems

The poems in this book were written after the form used by the 3rd century B.C. poet, Heraclitus, for his collection of poems believed to be called *Nightingales*. A friend of Heraclitus' and fellow poet, Callimachus of Cyrene, wrote the following epitaph for him when he died, sometime between 300 and 260 B.C.:

> *Heraclitus*
> —Callimachus
>
> They told me, Heraclitus, they told me you were dead,
> They brought me bitter news to hear and bitter tears to shed.
> I wept as I remember'd how often you and I
> Had tired the sun with talking and sent him down the sky.
>
> And now that thou art lying, my dear old Carian guest,
> A handful of grey ashes, long, long ago at rest,
> Still are thy pleasant voices, thy nightingales, awake;
> For Death, he taketh all away, but them he cannot take.
>
> Translated by William Cory

The only known poem remaining of Heraclitus' work, "The soil is freshly dug," appears in translation below:

"The soil is freshly dug"*

The soil is freshly dug, the half-faded wreaths of leaves
    droop across the face of the tombstone.
What do the letters say, traveller? What can they tell you
    of the smooth bones the slab says it guards?

"Stranger, I am Aretemias of Cnidus. I was the wife
    of Euphro. Labour-pains were not withheld
from me. I left one twin to guide my husband's old age,
    and took the other to remind me of him."

                                          Translated by Edwin Morgan

*Reprinted from *Collected Translations*, by Edwin Morgan, by permission of Carcanet Press.

Welcome the Birds

Through the gloom of early evening, a crane scratches
   mud into the folds of her feathers.
The pine savanna closes in. The humidity
   sweeps the wiregrass and ghosts, like vapor, rise.
"Phantoms, gathered here, come closer. We will dance and weep
   our sorrows into this ground. We will be
alone and together. We will remember and forget.
   Join this widening circle. Shout."

M_____

Here is the earth that holds you, a wooden cross hides
   under the rush of a downstream river
more permanent even than dirt. Who walks here at night?
   What do they see unexposed to the sun?
"Guest, I am M_____, still a slave
   of Ferguson. As a woman, numbered,
without a name, I raised his family and fed my
   daughter the letters of his alphabet."

Georgianna

The gravel of this road and the signpost, half bent
   from hundreds of storms and neglect,
mark a distance to a town I don't know. Where was I
   heading? The property of no one.
"Traveler above me, hear me. Alone in the dark,
   hidden and scared, I too, lost my way. The sign,
a mystery. I sang to myself and the heartbeat,
   whose rhythm is still my song's cadence."

Emily Harrison

I miss the terra cotta earth where I was born
   to a mother who only knew me five years,
raped by a man who would never know either of us.
   In my soul, I feel her lullaby;
sing it to my own child I never knew. "Way down
   yonder, down in the meadow…the poor
wee thing cried for her mammy…"* Her birth
   took my last breath, but left all my love.

*From the lullaby "All the Pretty Little Horses"

Abby Anderson

The ground is solid now—no flowers, wreaths, or trees have
   ever hid the words etched onto the marble.
What do the pictures mean, wanderer? Can they tell you
   of the stranger guarded by the ghosts?
"Witness, I am Abby Anderson. I was the slave
   of Beaumont. In the youth of my short life,
I bore two sons. One lives with me in the house of my God;
   the other, we wait for eternally."

She Whom the Worms Loved

Earthworms languish over dry, cracked, once-mud—
   holding an early morning vigil.
Whose name do they moan through the dust? Do they wait for
        the rain
   to relieve their undisturbed dwindling?
"Creatures above me, keep your wishes to yourself. I have wanted
   this day. Long years have passed and kept me tired
without joy. You will help my passage to the next life.
   Let us meet Oya* at the gates together."

*Oya is the Undergoddess of the Niger River who guards the underworld in Yoruba mythology.

Little Mary

Frost makes needles of the grey-green grass—all that is left
   to mark where I died. She, hoping to save me,
sent me to darkness. Mother, what did you call me?
   How did your bruised legs bend to the task?
"Child, you were the breath of my heartache, the shiver
   of hope disappeared. What could I give you?
Before you, I had two others whose fates I did not know.
   Join me in springtime—on the other side."

Katie

The morning glories, dormant on dew soft soil, untwist
    to the quiet dawn, the light their beacon.
Whose breath is the wind on these petals? Can she know
    what these flowers conceal? What visions they reveal?
"Visitor, these blossoms are the babies I couldn't have.
    The pain of none matched my quiet relief.
Barren, I worked the fields until I could no longer.
    In life I was alone, but not in death."

Rebecca

From the rocky shore, over lapping waves, you can hear
   the wailing cries of loneliness. Desperate
sounds to welcome company. Where does the weeping start?
   Whose eyes empty into this muddy river?
"Drifter, I am someone's memory. In life, I loved
   a husband and our three children. Sold
and separated, the agony too much to bear, I
   sank into the silence of the Mississippi."

Mother Shaw

A smell of constant decay seeps up from these marshlands
   and mosquitoes keep busy in the tall grass.
Far away from the fecund fields and sunlight off white rows
   of cotton, things are private here, muffled.
"Take note, no one. Water has disintegrated
   the flesh of my flesh, who I smothered
here, half a year into her pathetic life. The only
   good thing I ever did with my own."

Another Woman, 42

The forest depths have all but faded into a few trees
   and the wind's whispers haunt their leaves.
What can you gain, seeker, from the earthworm-polished bones,
   buried under this oak? What hope is left to recover?
"Trespasser, I am another unable to share her name.
   Alive, I hid so long in shadows,
I grew accustomed to the dark—lost any need for light.
   Born into dusk, I rest forever in shade."

Annie

Lost here, in this forest, the wide arms of trees shading
   my memories among the brown and green
undergrowth, I can speak to the leaves and pine needles
   cushioning my walk here, which was her walk here.
"Close by, your whisper holds me captive when the buzz
   of cicadas is a storm around me.
I raised your grandma till I could no longer. Watched her
   when she left. Laughed with her on her journey."

Liz Glodek lives and works in the Midwest. Her work has appeared in several journals including *The Greensboro Review, Lumina, North American Review* (finalist for the James Hearst Poetry Prize), *The North,* and *Janus Head*. She received her MFA from Sarah Lawrence College where she also founded the SLC Poetry Festival. She is an instructor at Simpson College.

www.ingramcontent.com/pod-product-compliance
Lightning Source LLC
Chambersburg PA
CBHW060228050426
42446CB00013B/3220